You've Got a Friend

Other books by

Blue Mountain Press INC

Come Into the Mountains, Dear Friend
by Susan Polis Schutz
I Want to Laugh, I Want to Cry
by Susan Polis Schutz
Peace Flows from the Sky
by Susan Polis Schutz
Someone Else to Love
by Susan Polis Schutz
I'm Not That Kind of Girl
by Susan Polis Schutz
Yours If You Ask
by Susan Polis Schutz
The Best Is Yet to Be
Step to the Music You Hear, Vol. I
The Language of Friendship
The Language of Love
The Language of Happiness
The Desiderata of Happiness
by Max Ehrmann
Whatever Is, Is Best
by Ella Wheeler Wilcox
Poor Richard's Quotations
by Benjamin Franklin
I Care About Your Happiness
by Kahlil Gibran/Mary Haskell
My Life and Love Are One
by Vincent Van Gogh
I Wish You Good Spaces
by Gordon Lightfoot
We Are All Children Searching for Love
by Leonard Nimoy
Come Be with Me
by Leonard Nimoy
Catch Me with Your Smile
by Peter McWilliams
Creeds to Love and Live By
On the Wings of Friendship
Think of Me Kindly
by Ludwig van Beethoven
With You There and Me Here
I Want You to Be Happy
by Hoyt Axton
The Dawn of Friendship
Once Only
by jonivan
Expressing Our Love
Just the Way I Am
Dolly Parton

You've Got a Friend

Poetic selections from the songs of

Carole King

Edited by Susan Polis Schutz,
with Illustrations by Stephen Schutz

Blue Mountain Press ™

Boulder, Colorado

Library of Congress Number: 78-59095
ISBN: 0-88396-030-3

Manufactured in the United States of America

Lyrics reprinted with permission from
Screen Gems-EMI Music, Inc. and Colgems-EMI Music, Inc.,
Hollywood, Ca.
Layout and design by SandPiper Studios, Inc.

First Printing: September, 1978
Second Printing: February, 1979

Blue Mountain Press INC.

P.O. Box 4549, Boulder, Colorado 80306

ACKNOWLEDGMENTS
"All you have to do," from the song *Some Kind of Wonderful*, by Carole King and Gerry Goffin. Copyright © 1961 Screen Gems-Columbia Music, Inc.
"Do the things," from the song *In The Name of Love*, by Carole King. Copyright © 1977 Colgems-EMI Music, Inc.
"Each of us," from the song *One*, by Carole King. Copyright © 1977 Colgems-EMI Music, Inc.
"Here we are," from the song *Time Alone*, by Carole King. Copyright © 1977 Colgems-EMI Music, Inc.
"I know how alone," from the song *Goodbye Don't Mean I'm Gone*, by Carole King. Copyright © 1972 Colgems Music Corp.
"I'll never forget you," from the song *So Much Love*, by Carole King and Gerry Goffin. Copyright © 1966 Screen Gems-Columbia Music, Inc.
"I'd like to know you better," from the song *I'd Like to Know You Better*, by Carole King. Copyright © 1975 Colgems Music Corp.
"Just as surely," from the song *Surely*, by Carole King. Copyright © 1971 Colgems Music Corp.
"Only love," from the song *Only Love Is Real*, by Carole King. Copyright © 1975 Colgems Music Corp.
"Simple things," from the song *Simple Things*, by Carole King and Rick Evers. Copyright © 1977 Colgems-EMI Music, Inc.
"Sitting here," from the song *What Am I Gonna Do*, by Carole King and Toni Stern. Copyright © 1970 Colgems Music Corp.
"Sometimes I wonder," from the song *Home Again*, by Carole King. Copyright © 1971 Colgems Music Corp.
"The winds of time," from the song *To Know That I Love You*, by Carole King. Copyright © 1977 Colgems-EMI Music, Inc.
"There are those," from the song *To Love*, by Carole King and Gerry Goffin. Copyright © 1970 Screen Gems-Columbia Music, Inc.
"Tonight you're mine," from the song *Will You Love Me Tomorrow*, by Carole King and Gerry Goffin. Copyright © 1960, 1961 Screen Gems-Columbia Music, Inc.
"Wanting you," from the song *Where You Lead*, by Carole King and Toni Stern. Copyright © 1971 Colgems Music Corp.
"We've been putting," from the song *It's Gonna Work Out Fine*, by Carole King. Copyright © 1975 Colgems Music Corp.
"We've seen the seasons," from the song *The Best Is Yet To Come*, by Carole King and Dave Palmer. Copyright © 1974 Colgems Music Corp.
"We have so much," from the song *So Many Ways*, by Carole King. Copyright © 1975 Colgems Music Corp.
"When you're down," from the song *You've Got A Friend*, by Carole King. Copyright © 1971 Colgems Music Corp.
"You just call," from the song *You've Got A Friend*, by Carole King. Copyright © 1971 Colgems Music Corp.
"You light up my life," from the song *You Light Up My Life*, by Carole King. Copyright © 1973 Colgems Music Corp.
"You make my day," from the song *Brighter*, by Carole King. Copyright © 1971 Colgems Music Corp.
"You're gentle to me," from the song *You Gentle Me*, by Carole King and Dave Palmer. Copyright © 1974 Colgems Music Corp.
"You're just time away," from the song *So Far Away*, by Carole King. Copyright © 1971 Colgems Music Corp.
"You've got to get up," from the song *Beautiful*, by Carole King. Copyright © 1971 Colgems Music Corp.
"Your love was the key," from the song *(You Make Me Feel Like A) Natural Woman*, by Carole King, Gerry Goffin and Jerry Wexler. Copyright © 1967 Screen Gems-Columbia Music, Inc.

Contents

"I've found my answer to life is living
The secret of living is life"

Carole King

Introduction

Some of the most vibrant and beautiful poetry to be found anywhere today is contained in the lyrics of contemporary music. Carole King distills the essence of poetic expression in her music. The tenderness and warmth of her lyrics is complemented by their easy rhythmic flow.

Carole's lyrics in *You've Got a Friend* span a period of almost twenty years, a reflection of the enduring spirit of her talent. They trace her own growth and change both as a woman and as an artist. Inherent in all her work is a loving gentleness and perception—a willingness to accept as well as the ability to change. These qualities have made Carole one of the most popular and versatile songwriters in contemporary music.

You've Got a Friend is a collection of Carole's most heartwarming lyrics, selected by Susan Polis Schutz and enhanced by the soft airbrush paintings of Stephen Schutz. Characterized by the strength and compassion that have made Carole King an influential force in the recording industry, *You've Got a Friend* is a glowing tribute to life and love and art.

You make my day
a little brighter
in every way
Some people live
in darkness
their whole life through
I just know that
I'd have been
one of them
if it hadn't been
for you

I'm so glad to have you
in this old troubled time
when true love and understanding ...
are so hard to find ...
I think of the loving good times
we've had, and I know
we're going to make it through
Because you make my day
a little brighter in every way

 imple things
mean a lot to me
Some things
  only children can see
Simple things
like horses running free
And easy acceptance of life

Simple things never compromise
All things have a rhythm I can realize
I feel content in my freedom
And I feel my freedom is right

I never want to stop being a child
I want to see the flowers growing wild
on the hillside
To see the sun rise in the morning
Sunlight growing filling the skies

Simple things of the earth don't die
They just grow and change as time goes by
There are no questions without answers
I've found my answer to life is living
The secret of living is life

I'd like to know you better
though I already feel as if I do
meeting you has been so good …
And if only temporarily
I want to be your friend …
I'd like to know you better

Sitting here
and thinking about you
so far away
wondering what
you're thinking
and wondering
what you'd say
if you were sitting
here beside me …
I love you
so much

You've got to
    get up
    every morning
    with a smile
        on your face
and show the world
all the love in your heart
Then people are going to treat
you better
You're going to find
yes, you will
That you're beautiful
as you feel

Waiting at the station
with a workday wind a' blowing
I've got nothing to do
but watch the passers by
Mirrored in their faces
I see frustration growing
And they don't see it showing
Why do I?

I have often
asked myself the reason
for the sadness
in a world where tears
are just a lullaby
If there's any answer
maybe love can end the madness
Maybe not, oh
but we can only try

You light up my life
like sunrise in the morning
You make me believe
anything is possible
I didn't have a dream
to my name ...
but you came to
light up my life
You brought me faith
and hope
and love
and light

With your tender smile
you brought me
to the promise
of life outside a world
of nine to five and Sunday
I didn't know how rich
I could be
until you gave your
love to me

Do the things
You believe in
In the name of love
And know that
You aren't alone
We all have doubts and fears

Know throughout every season
You are the name of love
And you'll keep on feeling at home
Throughout the coming years

Change is for certain
This we all know
Each day opening the curtain
On a brand new show

Through your sorrow and grieving
Don't forget the name of love
It goes on without any end
Forever

Birth and life and death
Make a circle
We are all part of
To see the light everlasting
Live in the name of love
Forever

Each of us is one —
All of us are one ...
Open your heart
and let the love
come shining through ...
He is one
She is one
A tree is one
The earth is one
The universe is one ...
I am one
We are one

Here we are
in time alone
No one else's
feelings
but our own
Seems to me that
we have always known
What love was meant to be

Separately we stood before
Life was good but we knew
there should be more
Time alone could open up the door
And you came through for me

No sign of the changes
we have come through
No mind of the strangers
who think they
know you

Now as one
we are a light
Though sometimes we were
blinded by the night
Here in time alone
it all seems right
And I'm feeling wholly free
Won't you stay
in time alone with me

**T**he winds of time
set my mind at ease
Like a gentle breeze
they let me know
that I love you
Over and over again
we light the flame
Rediscovering that we are the same
and I love you
Ah — it feels so good
to know that I love you
With each new morning
it's a good feeling to know
There is something
to look forward to these days

As time sets in
we still begin
to know each other
Even now as we go
our separate ways
Ever together
Like the sun and the moon
we give each other room
To shine and to glow
and to grow and I know
that I love you
Ah — it feels so good
to know that I love you

We've been
putting each other
through a hard time
And it's a mighty good feeling
to know we're going to
work it out ...
It's going to work out fine ...

Tonight
you're mine
completely
You give your love
so sweetly
Tonight the light of love
is in your eyes
But will you love me tomorrow?

Tonight with words unspoken
You say that I'm the only one
But will my heart be broken
when the night
meets the morning sun?

Is this a lasting treasure
or just a moment's pleasure?
Can I believe
the magic of your sighs?
Will you still love me tomorrow?

I have to know that your love
is love I can be sure of
So tell me now
and I won't ask again
Will you still love me tomorrow?

Only love is real
everything else illusion
adding to the confusion
of the way we contrive
to just stay alive
Tracing a line
'till we can define
the thing that allows
us to feel
Only love is real

You're gentle to me

When life seems
 so relentless
you gentle me
When my striving seems so senseless
you gentle me
You lift my spirits
I get higher by degree
when you're gentle to me

When tension's taking shape
When I feel the pressure building
and it's just too much to take
You touch the anxious need in me
with love ...

I'll never forget you
or what you've done
I'll never turn my back
on you for anyone
I've got so much love to give ...
enough to last
a whole life through

We've seen
the seasons
turning
As we weathered
every storm
And the climate of our loving
Is so tender and so warm

And the best is yet to come
This is only the beginning
And we've only just begun

Your love was the key
to my peace of mind ...
I'm no longer doubtful
of what I'm living for ...
If I make you happy
I don't need to do more

All you
have to do
is touch
my hand
to show me
you understand
and something
happens to me ...
Any time my
little world is blue
I just have to
look at you
and everything
seems to be
some kind of wonderful

I know I can't express
this feeling of tenderness
There's so much I want to say
but the right words
just don't come my way
I just know
when I'm in your embrace
this world is a happy place
and something happens to me

Sometimes I wonder
if I'm ever going to
make it home again
it's so far and out of sight
I really need someone
to talk to and nobody else
knows how to comfort me tonight
Snow is cold
rain is wet
Chills my soul
right to the marrow
I won't be happy
'till I see you alone again
'till I'm home again
and feeling right

Just as surely
as the sun
is going to rise
as the birds
are going to sing ...
as everything
is part of
everything
I'm a part
of you
and I
love you

There are
those of us
too cool
   for passion
They're the ones
that it could
do some good
And there are
those who say
it's out of fashion

they're the ones
who only wish
they could
To love, to love
to love ...
All you need's
the opportunity
to love ...
And I'm so glad
I found
you

Wanting you
the way I do
I only want
to be with you …
If anyone can
make me happy
you're the one
who can
Where you lead
I will follow …

We have
so much
in common
although
we come
from places worlds apart
When you reach out
and touch my hand
without a word ...
you're beautiful
You are in my heart ...

Since I've been spending ...
time with you
you've taught me something new
every day
And I just want to say
the music comes
from you and me
and it's plain to see
that we both know

So many ways
So many ways to show
you love someone
So many ways
So many ways to show
someone you care

You're just time away
Long ago I reached for you
and there you stood
Holding you again
could only do me good
How I wish I could ...

When you're
    down and
    troubled
and you need
    some love and care
and nothing, nothing is going right
Close your eyes and think of me
and soon I will be there
to brighten up even your darkest night

You just call out my name
and you know wherever I am
I'll come running
to see you again
Winter, spring, summer or fall
All you have to do is call
And I'll be there
You've got a friend

If the sky above you
grows dark and full of clouds
And that old north wind begins to blow
Keep your head together
and call my name out loud
Soon you'll hear me knocking at your door

You just call out my name
and you know wherever I am
I'll come running
to see you again
Winter, spring, summer or fall
All you have to do is call
And I'll be there
You've got a friend

Now ain't it good to know
that you've got a friend
when people can be so cold?
They'll hurt you
yes, and desert you
and take your soul if you let them
Oh, but don't you let them

You just call out my name
and you know wherever I am
I'll come running
to see you again
Winter, spring, summer or fall
All you have to do is call
And I'll be there
You've got a friend

I know how alone you are
... it's so hard
to be so far
from the ones
who mean the most to you
when you would
so much rather
have them close ...
You know
my love is always there

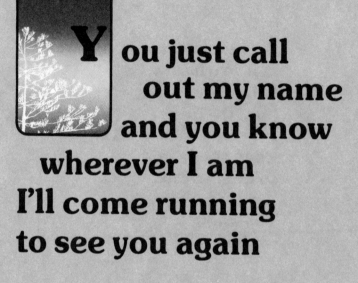

You just call
out my name
and you know
wherever I am
I'll come running
to see you again

Winter, spring
summer or fall
All you have to do is call
And I'll be there
You've got a friend

About the Author

Any book written on the history of popular music over the past twenty years is bound to include a chapter on Carole King. Her continuing influence on the recording industry has been nothing less than remarkable. Born in Brooklyn, New York, Carole entered the world of professional music in 1958, when she recorded several records for ABC-Paramount.

With Carole composing the music and Gerry Goffin writing the lyrics, the two were soon to become one of the hottest teams in the mushrooming business of rock and roll. Carole's early hits include songs like "Locomotion," "Will You Love Me Tomorrow," "Chains," "Up on the Roof" and "Natural Woman," recorded by such artists as the Beatles, Tony Orlando, the Shirelles, Bobby Vee, and Aretha Franklin. During the early sixties, barely a week passed when a Goffin/King tune was not high on the charts.

Throughout the decade, Carole continued to write and compose songs, releasing several albums of her own and creating hits for numerous other groups. In 1971 came what seemed to be the culmination of years and years of working, reworking and polishing her style: Carole's record-breaking *Tapestry* album was released.

Tapestry won four Grammy awards and still retains the honor of being one of the best-selling albums in music history. As in all of Carole's work, its appeal lies in the honesty and compassion of its gentle lyrics and in its perception of life, self and love.

Today Carole continues to work on her music, constantly developing and experimenting, always growing. "I am a person like anyone else. I put my heart, soul and mind out there—that's what I'd like to share with the people, the public. I give them everything in the music. The music, to me, is what it's all about."